SUPER CUTE!

Baby Hedgehogs

by Megan Borgert-Spaniol

BLASTOFF! READERS

BELLWETHER MEDIA • MINNEAPOLIS, MN

Note to Librarians, Teachers, and Parents:

Blastoff! Readers are carefully developed by literacy experts and combine standards-based content with developmentally appropriate text.

Level 1 provides the most support through repetition of high-frequency words, light text, predictable sentence patterns, and strong visual support.

Level 2 offers early readers a bit more challenge through varied simple sentences, increased text load, and less repetition of high-frequency words.

Level 3 advances early-fluent readers toward fluency through increased text and concept load, less reliance on visuals, longer sentences, and more literary language.

Level 4 builds reading stamina by providing more text per page, increased use of punctuation, greater variation in sentence patterns, and increasingly challenging vocabulary.

Level 5 encourages children to move from "learning to read" to "reading to learn" by providing even more text, varied writing styles, and less familiar topics.

Whichever book is right for your reader, Blastoff! Readers are the perfect books to build confidence and encourage a love of reading that will last a lifetime!

This edition first published in 2016 by Bellwether Media, Inc.

No part of this publication may be reproduced in whole or in part without written permission of the publisher. For information regarding permission, write to Bellwether Media, Inc., Attention: Permissions Department, 5357 Penn Avenue South, Minneapolis, MN 55419.

Library of Congress Cataloging-in-Publication Data

Borgert-Spaniol, Megan, 1989- author.
  Baby Hedgehogs / by Megan Borgert-Spaniol.
    pages cm. – (Blastoff! Readers. Super Cute!)
  Summary: "Developed by literacy experts for students in kindergarten through grade three, this book introduces baby hedgehogs to young readers through leveled text and related photos"– Provided by publisher.
  Audience: Ages 5-8
  Audience: K to grade 3
  Includes bibliographical references and index.
  ISBN 978-1-62617-217-3 (hardcover: alk. paper)
  1. Hedgehogs–Infancy–Juvenile literature. 2. Hedgehogs–Juvenile literature. I. Title. II. Series: Blastoff! Readers. 1, Super Cute!
  QL737.E753B67 2016
  599.33'2-dc23
                      2015009728

Printed in the United States of America, North Mankato, MN.

Table of Contents

Hoglets!

Baby hedgehogs are called hoglets. Most **litters** have 4 to 7 hoglets.

Hoglets have
no hair at birth.
Their backs are
covered in short,
soft **spines**.

spines

Newborn hoglets stay safe in a nest of grass and leaves.

The babies drink mom's milk. They all line up to **nurse**.

Out of the Nest

Hoglets leave the nest after a few weeks. Now their spines are long and sharp.

They follow mom around. She shows them how to search for **insects**.

Soon the hoglets are on their own. They watch for badgers and other **predators**.

All Curled Up

A hoglet curls into a ball when in danger. This makes the baby hard to attack.

A hoglet also
curls up to sleep.
All tucked in!

Glossary

insects—small animals with six legs and hard outer bodies; insect bodies are divided into three parts.

litters—groups of babies that are born together

newborn—just recently born

nurse—to drink mom's milk

predators—animals that hunt other animals for food

spines—hair-like spikes that grow on the backs of hedgehogs

To Learn More

AT THE LIBRARY

Rissman, Rebecca. *Hedgehogs: Nocturnal Foragers*. Chicago, Ill.: Heinemann Library, 2015.

Schuetz, Kari. *Hedgehogs*. Minneapolis, Minn.: Bellwether Media, 2013.

Wellesley, Rosie. *The Very Helpful Hedgehog*. London, U.K.: Pavilion Children's, 2012.

ON THE WEB

Learning more about hedgehogs is as easy as 1, 2, 3.

1. Go to www.factsurfer.com.

2. Enter "hedgehogs" into the search box.

3. Click the "Surf" button and you will see a list of related web sites.

With factsurfer.com, finding more information is just a click away.

Index